M000044204

"And as powerful as our memories are, our dreams must be even stronger, for when our memories outweigh our dreams we become old, and it is the eternal destiny of America to remain forever young, always reaching beyond, always becoming as our founders pledged a more appropriate union."

—At the Millennium Gala Event. Reported in the *Washington Post*. January 1st, 2000.

"But today the dominant message from this administration is,

'you're on your own.'"

—To early for a plug? Cleveland, Ohio. May 21st, 1992.

The

Rants, Raves **&** THOUGHTS of

BILL CLINTON

THE PRESIDENT IN HIS OWN WORDS + THOSE OF OTHERS

{William J. Clinton}

Publisher
Jeff Brauer

Project Manager
Michael Buening

Writer and Editor
Paul Roer

Illustrator
Eric Chun

Contributing Editors:

Chaitanya Rao and Chris Evans

ON YOUR OWN PUBLICATIONS, LLC
Corporate Address:
Brooklyn Navy Yard
Building 120, Suite 207
Brooklyn, NY 11205

Tel: 718.875.9455
Fax: 772.673.2436
Web: www.oyobooks.com

© 2002
On Your Own Publications, LLC

1-929377-56-8

Bill Clinton, née William Jefferson Blythe IV, emerged from his mama's womb on August 19th, 1946 in Hope, Arkansas. His father was killed in a car accident three months before his birth and he was raised mostly by his grandparents during the first years of his life. His mother reclaimed him after returning from a nursing school and introduced a new paterfamilias, Roger Clinton, a Buick salesman with a thin mustache and violent penchant to drink and beat, from whom Bill eventually took his less WASP-y surname. Bill's biggest adolescent success came when he was sent to Boy's Nation by the American Legion and had the honor to shake John F. Kennedy's hand.

He attended Georgetown University where he studied international affairs and then took his studies to Oxford with pockets full of Rhodes scholarship money and a driving passion to learn the secret recipe for Branston Pickle. Having not inhaled limey marijuana, he came back to the U.S. and entered Yale Law school where he met Hillary Rodham. They married on October 11th, 1975.

In 1978, Clinton became Arkansas' and the nation's youngest and sexiest governor—a seductive 32 years old. He was not reelected to a second term, but regained the governorship a few years later and held it until 1992, when he defeated Ross Perot and George Bush to become the 42nd President of the United States.

Clinton's reign as supreme commander of the universe had its ups and downs. On the one hand, he was the second president, ever, to be impeached, on the other hand, he didn't bald much. In his first term, Bill Clinton was able to pull the U.S. out of a sluggish economy, significantly reduce the deficit, complete NAFTA, shut down the federal government, and bomb the shit out of Bosnia. Not bad for a sweet talkin' Democrat.

The end of Bill's first term marked the beginning of his downfall when the Whitewater scandal erupted, an investigation into alleged misdeeds concerning an Arkansas land deal. He was still able to defeat Bob Dole by a decent margin to gain a second term in 1996, but the next four years proved to be a giant crick-in-the-neck for Bill. Kenneth Starr's investigation into Whitewater unearthed a relationship between Bill Clinton and White House intern, Monica "Lips" Lewinsky. Bill twisted and turned his words in court and in public only to find himself charged with perjury, obstruction of justice, and abuse of power. Bill admitted to a grand jury in August 1998 of being involved in an "inappropriate relationship" with "Lips" but promised never-ever to do it again. He was impeached. The Senate could not come up with the vote to oust Clinton, so he had to remain president for the remaining year and a half, spending more time scooping up Buddy's poo-poo than making out with his wife. Them's the breaks.

BUBBA—LICIOUS

opening hodgepodge

"Let's

do it."

—When asked if he was ready to start the Q and A.
Remarks on Shanghai Radio. June 30th, 1998.

"As President, it is my duty to speak frankly to the American people about the world in which we now live."

—And it's big and blue and covered with sugary, whip-cream stuff called 'clouds'. Upon signing the NAFTA side agreements. The East Room. September 14th, 1993.

"And as powerfu

"I haven't eaten at a McDonald's since I became President."

—Holier Than Thou on NBC's *Meet the Press*. Reported in the *Chicago Tribune*. November 10th, 1997.

"You can put wings on a pig,
  but you don't make it an eagle."

—Pre-evoking George W. Bush and commenting on the welfare
bill. Reported in the *Pittsburgh Post-Gazette*. August 9th, 1996.

"Nobody

who wasn't a high-energy physicist had even heard of the World Wide Web when I became president. And, now, even my cat, Socks, has his own page."

—140 hits already this year. Giving graduation speech at Princeton. Reported in the *St. Petersburg Times*. June 5th, 1996.

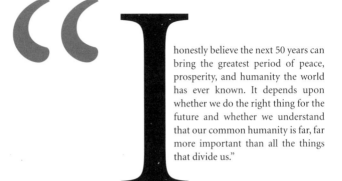

"I honestly believe the next 50 years can bring the greatest period of peace, prosperity, and humanity the world has ever known. It depends upon whether we do the right thing for the future and whether we understand that our common humanity is far, far more important than all the things that divide us."

—At Carelton College. June 10th, 2000.

"If a President of the United States ever lied to the American people he should resign."

—Bet yer bottom dollar? Commenting on Nixon and Watergate.
Reported in the *Arkansas Gazette*. August 8th, 1974.

"In some nations, people are pessimistic, and in all nations some people are pessimistic, and in all nations there are people with difficulties."

—Riiiiiiiiiiight…At the G-7 Jobs Conference. Detroit, Michigan. March 14th, 1994.

"If you are President of the United States at a time when everything is kind of going haywire and changing, you cannot always do what is popular and be right. Sometimes you have to do what's going to be right in 10 or 20 years. That's what you have to do."

—At the Florida Presidential Gala. September 15th, 1995.

"The road to tyranny, we must never forget, begins with the destruction of the truth."

—And ends with biscotti and espresso.
University of Connecticut. October 15th, 1995.

"Ten years ago this month, the Berlin Wall tumbled, a curtain lifted across Europe. The best way to celebrate that anniversary is to rekindle the feeling of liberation for a new generation."

—"So let us all drop our pants and sing 'Hallelujah.'"
Addressing the Turkish Grand National Assembly. November 15th, 1999.

"This is always an important day for our country… it is an unusual and, I think, unusually important day today. I may not be quite as easy with my words today as I have been in years past, and I was up rather late last night thinking about and praying about what I ought to say today. And rather unusual for me, I actually tried to write it down. So if you will forgive me, I will do my best to say what it is I want to say to you—and I may have to take my glasses out to read my own writing."

—Go back three years from the attacks. 9:40am. At a breakfast with religious leaders. The East Room. September 11th, 1998.

"When I was in England
   I experimented with marijuana
  a time or two,
and I didn't like it. I didn't inhale."

—But in Amsterdam, it was all hookers and hash.
Reported in the *New York Times*. March 30th, 1992.

"I'll take both of you, but only one at a time."

—When interviewing new White House interns... no no... when asked simultaneous questions at a press conference with Tony Blair. May 29th, 1997.

"You know my favorite joke about the guy that falls off the edge of the Grand Canyon? He's falling and he sees this little twig on the edge of the canyon and he grabs it. And the roots start coming out and he realizes he's going to fall again, and he says, "God, why me? I am a good man. I work hard, I pay my taxes, I take care of my family. I'm a good citizen, why me?" This thunderous voice says, "Son, there's just something about you I don't like."

—Bill Clinton on the right–wing element that was still after him after he left office. *Newsweek*. April 8th, 2002.

"I believe that

the greatness of nations in the 21st century will be defined not by whether they can dictate to millions and millions of people within and beyond their borders, but instead by whether they can provide their citizens, without regard to their race or their gender, the opportunity to live up to the fullest of their ability, to take full advantage of the incredible things that are in the world of today and tomorrow."

—Like Aspergum. Live telecast to the Russian people. Moscow. January 14th, 1994.

QUESTION If a person touched another person— you touched another person on the breasts, would that be, in your view, and was it within your view, when you took the deposition, within the definition of sexual relations?

CLINTON If the person being deposed—in this case me—directly touched the breasts of another person, with the purpose to arouse or gratify, under that definition, that would be included.

QUESTION Only directly, sir, or would it be directly or through clothes?

CLINTON Well, I would I think the common—sense definition would be directly. That's how I would infer what it means.

QUESTION If the person being deposed kissed the breasts of another person, would that be in the definition of sexual relations as you understood it when you were under oath in the Jones case?

CLINTON Yes, that would constitute contact. I think that would, if it were direct contact.

QUESTION And you testified that you didn't have sexual relations with Monica Lewinsky in the Jones deposition, under that definition, correct?

CLINTON That's correct, sir.

Grand Jury testimony. August 17th, 1998.

"Martin Sheen

is the only American president that's not term–limited. So he's got real influence, unlike Dole and me, he's still got the job and so he can do it."

—"Here's my headshot in case Martin gets canned."
On *Larry King Live*. September 3rd, 2002.

"On behalf of our nation, I salute my predecessor,
President Bush, for his half–century of service to America."

—First Inaugural Address. January 20th, 1993.

"Hillary, Chelsea and I join all Americans in wishing our
very best to the next president, George W. Bush, to his
family and his administration in meeting these
challenges and in leading freedom's
march in this new century."

—Clinton's legacy—meat in a Bush sandwich. His farewell speech. January 19th, 2001.

"Usually briefs."

—When asked what type of underwear he prefers: boxers or briefs. MTV's *Enough is Enough*. April 19th, 1994.

"I want to say a special word of thanks to the fine people who work in this peach program and to the people who participate in it, not only to those who are here with me but those with whom I met behind this building in the play yard."

—And remember, nobody likes a tattle tale. Speaking at the Clayton County Office of Family and Children's Services. September 11th, 1992.

"**Reporter:** A lot of Americans are not wildly pronuclear and thought the U.S. may have overreacted in past years in its very heavy–handed treatment of New Zealand. Would you consider meeting now with a New Zealand leader and discussing the situation? Isn't there some way that a compromise can be reached so you can agree to disagree, but still restore the political and security relationship?

The President: I've given absolutely no thought to that question. And I'm afraid if I give an answer to it, I'll be in more trouble tomorrow than I can figure out."

—"Too busy openin' up this fortune cookie." Press conference at the White House. June 17th, 1993.

"The other thing we have to do is to take seriously
the role in this problem of…
older men who prey on underage women….
There are consequences to decisions and…
one way or another,
people always wind up being held accountable."

—Sometimes it's just too obvious. In a speech endorsing a national effort against teen pregnancy. Reported in *U.S. News and World Report*. June 13th, 1996.

"When I was a younger man and had a life, I owned an El Camino pickup in the '70s. It was a real sort of Southern deal. I had Astroturf in the back."

—"They called me 'El Vato' and I could really tear it up." Speech to employees at a GM factory. Shreveport, Louisiana. February 8th, 1994.

"African–Americans

"Because I won. You have to understand that they thought there would never be another Democratic president. They thought that they had found a fool–proof formula to turn us into cardboard cutouts, superficial one–dimensional non–American figures to the American people… they had this little formula. And so we didn't fit the formula, and the American people voted for me. And they never thought it was legitimate… They decided no honeymoon, no nothing, you know, 'We should not have ever lost the White House, it's ours. It belongs to us.' And you're laughing, but I'm telling you, this is true. I never would have believed it if I hadn't lived through it."

—When asked why the right wing despised him so. UC Berkeley. January 29th, 2002.

watch the same news at night that ordinary Americans do."

—On colored, no no, black and white, no no… on TV. Aired on Black Entertainment Television. November 2nd, 1994.

"From this joyful mountaintop of celebration, we hear a call to service in the valley. We have heard the trumpets. We have changed the guard. And now, each in our own way, and with God's help, we must answer the call."

—Break out the nacho cheese dip! First Inaugural Address. January 20th, 1993.

"An unbelievable

rewriting of history."

—Like what they do in parochial school textbooks. What Clinton called reports of his draft—dodging. *Insight on the News*. March 23rd, 1998.

THIS LAND IS CLIN-TON AND (GORE) LAND

on America

There is nothing wrong with America that cannot be cured with what is right in America."

—Except athlete's foot. 1st Inaugural Address. January 20th, 1993.

"

I'm glad to be in a conversation where the American people think someone else is pulling a fast one on them instead of the President."

—In an interview on ESPN Radio. March 25th, 1995.

"The United States

cannot turn our back on the world, nor can other nations. I know our engagement costs money and sometimes it costs lives. I know well that we cannot solve every problem, nor should we try. But in an era of change and opportunity and peril, America must be willing to assume the obligations and the risks of leadership. And I am determined to see that we do that."

—Atlanta, Georgia. May 3rd, 1994.

"We are going through a period of change as profound as anything that's happened in this country in a hundred years. This is like when we moved from being a rural agricultural country into being an industrial urbanized country. Now we're going from being an industrial economy to a high–technology, information–based economy. We're going from the Cold War relationships in our global foreign policy to a global economy, where we're becoming integrated economically and there are all kinds of pressures for disintegration—disintegration of families, of communities, of national economic policy—and the growth of extremism all over the world, political and religious and ethnic extremism."

—Miami, Florida. September 19th, 1995.

"The United States is a nation of immigrants and a nation of laws."

—And a nation of shitty immigration laws. Press conference with President Zedillo of Mexico. October 5th, 1995.

"No American

will ever be able to seriously say again, 'My vote doesn't count.'"

—Save for thousands of Floridians. Reported in *New York Newsday*. November 9th, 2000.

"I would like them to say I restored a sense of hope and optimism to my country, that I strengthened the economy, and made it possible for my people to lead the world economically into the 21st century and that I restored the sense of community in America; that we came back together as a people, even though we are very diverse now. And I would like it to be said that I helped lead the world to more peaceful cooperation, into a future very different from the bloody and divided past of the 20th century."

—Dreams can come true, it can happen to you. Maaaaaaaaaybe not. When asked what he'd like the historians to say about him. Live telecast to the Russian people. Moscow. January 14th, 1994.

"So that's it.

I feel pretty good about the future of this country, and you should, too. This is a very great country. We go through difficult periods from time to time. We will always have some bad people, as any society does. There will always be a measure of tragedy, as is the lot of human nature, as the Scripture teaches us. But America is coming back together. America is moving forward economically. But America dare not forget that our children are the future of this country."

—At the National Leadership Forum of Community Anti–Drug Coalitions. Washington, DC. November 2nd, 1995.

"We can't be so fixated on our desire to preserve the rights of ordinary Americans…"

—Only the SuperAmericans created in secret labs in Alexandria.
Reported in *USA Today*. March 11th, 1993.

"I want to be a president for every man, woman, and child in this country. But that means we all have to be Americans again, not just getting but giving, not just placing blame but taking responsibility, not just looking out for ourselves but looking out for each other. I believe with all my heart and soul that Americans want to be part of a country that brings out the best in us, not the worst."

—Statement used in an op–ed piece. November 2nd, 1992.

"No less today than five decades ago, our destinies are joined. For America the commitment to our common future is not an option, it is a necessity. We are closing the door on the 20th century, a century that saw humanity at its worst and at its most noble. Here, today, let us dedicate ourselves to working together to make the new century a time when partnership between America and Europe lifts the lives of all the people of the world."

—Commemorative event for the 50th anniversary of the Marshall Plan. The Hague, Netherlands. May 28, 1997.

"No less
our des
the com
future is
We are
century.

oday than five decades
nies are joined. For Ame
nitment to our common
not an option, it is a nec
osing the door on the 20
century that saw huma

"You know the one thing that's wrong with this country?

Everyone gets a chance to have their fair say."

—Promoting his Fascism initiative to the beat of James Brown's "I Feel Good."
Reported in the *Houston Chronicle*. May 29th, 1993.

"My vision is that in the 21st century this country will be a high–opportunity place, where we are growing entrepreneurs and growing the middle class and shrinking the under class; where we have good schools and good health care systems and safe streets and a clean environment; where people have the opportunity to make the most of their own lives and families and communities have a chance to solve their own problems, and America is a force for freedom and prosperity and peace throughout the world. That is my vision."

—On his view of 21st century America, at the Florida Presidential Gala. Miami, Florida. September 15th, 1995.

QUESTION If Monica Lewinsky says that while you were in the Oval Office area you touched her breasts, would she be lying?

CLINTON That is not my recollection. My recollection is that I did not have sexual relations with Ms. Lewinsky. And I'm staying on my former statement about that.

QUESTION If she says that you kissed her breast, would she be lying?

CLINTON I'm going to revert to my former statement.

QUESTION OK. If Monica Lewinsky says that, while you were in the Oval Office area you touched her genitalia, would she be lying? That calls for a yes, no, or reverting to your former statement.

CLINTON I will revert to my statement on that.

Grand Jury testimony. August 17th, 1998.

"So with profound gratitude for the defense of the Constitution and the best in America that was raised today by the members here and those who joined them, I ask the American people to move with me—to go on from here to rise above the rancor, to overcome the pain and division, to be a repairer of the breach—all of us—to make this country as one America what it can and must be for our children in the new century about to dawn."

—Statement after his impeachment. December 20th, 1998.

"Each and every one of us, in our own way, must assume personal responsibility—not only for ourselves and our families, but for our neighbors and our nation. Our greatest responsibility is to embrace a new spirit of community for a new century. For any one of us to succeed, we must succeed as one America."

—Second Inaugural Address. January 20th, 1997.

ach

WILLIAM TELL

on investigation and

impeachment

"I have absolutely leveled

"I believe any person who asks for forgiveness has to be prepared to give it."

—When asked if, in his heart, he can forgive and forget. Response to his acquittal in the Senate on the articles of impeachment. February 12th, 1999.

"Even presidents have private lives. It is time to stop the pursuit of personal destruction and the prying into private lives and get on with our national life."

—Amen! Now break out the bubbly. Address to the nation. August 18th, 1998.

with the American people."

—Jivin' on *60 Minutes* about, among other things, infidelities in his past. Reported in *The Plain Dealer*. September 13th, 1998.

"Don't we make a beautiful couple—

beauty and

the beast."

—The come–on Clinton allegedly used with Paula Jones, according to her lawsuit. In an official response, the president's lawyers claimed he had "no recollection of ever meeting or speaking with Paula Jones," and thus denied ever making the statement. Reported in the *Boston Globe*. October 20, 1998.

"I tried to walk a line between acting lawfully and testifying falsely,

"Well, I've got to do my best. You know, I'd be—I'd be less than candid if I said it was, you know, just hunky–dory. You know, these—but I've been living with this sort of thing for a long time. And my experience has been, unfortunately, sometimes, you know, when one charge dies, another one just lifts up to take its place."

—Maybe if you kept it in your pants… *The News Hour with Jim Lehrer.* January 21st, 1998.

but I now realize that I did not fully accomplish that goal."

—Thank bejesus you didn't succeed. A released statement on the independent council's investigation. January 19th, 2001.

"I answered their questions truthfully,
including questions about my private life,
questions no American citizen would ever want to answer."

—"Hooey, now everybody knows I wipe boogers under the desk
in the Oval Office." Address to the Nation. August 18th, 1998.

"No one

wants to get this matter behind us more than I do, except maybe all the rest of the American people."

—Come on, Bill, the American people live off this kinda shit. The Rose Garden. July 31st, 1998.

"Now that the Senate has fulfilled its constitutional responsibility, bringing this process to a conclusion, I want to say again to the American people how profoundly sorry I am for what I said and did to trigger these events and the great burden they have imposed on the Congress and the American people."

—Heeeeeeee Hawwwwww! Response to his acquittal in the Senate on the articles of impeachment. February 12th, 1999.

"So I will admit this, sir.

My goal in this deposition was to be truthful, but not particularly helpful. I did not wish to do the work of the Jones' lawyers. I deplored what they were doing. I deplored the innocent people they were tormenting and traumatizing…. But I was determined to walk through the minefield of this deposition without violating the law. And I believe I did."

—Grand Jury testimony. August 17th, 1998.

I'm just tryi

"I'm just trying to suppress my natural impulses

and

get back to work."

—Which include stickin' it in fat and ugly chicks.
The News Hour with Jim Lehrer. January 21st, 1998.

ig to supple

"Presidents are people, too."

—Cry baby–ing at a joint news conference with President Jacques Chirac of France,
facing the press for the first time since his impeachment trial. February 19th, 1999.

"The question is, what are we going to do now? I have accepted responsibility for what I did wrong in my personal life, and I have invited members of Congress to work with us to find a reasonable bipartisan and proportionate response. That approach was rejected today by Republicans in the House, but I hope it will be embraced by the Senate. I hope there will be a constitutional and fair means of resolving this matter in a prompt manner. Meanwhile, I will continue to do the work of the American people. We still, after all, have to save Social Security and Medicare for the 21st century."

—Statement after his impeachment. December 20th, 1998.

"Well, you might—in my view, that is something that you have to demonstrate every day. My opinion is not as important as the opinion of others. What is important is that I do my job… I'm determined to lead this country and to focus on the issues that are before us. It is not an option. There's no option."

—When asked if he thinks he has the moral authority to lead this nation. Reported in the *New York Times*. September 16th, 1998.

"I also am humbled and very grateful for the support and the prayers I have received from millions of Americans over this past year. Now I ask all Americans, and I hope all Americans—here in Washington and throughout our land—will rededicate ourselves to the work of serving our nation and building our future together."

—Response to his acquittal in the Senate on the articles of impeachment. February 12th, 1999.

illions of Americans over this past year. Now I ask all Americans, and I
's to the work of serving our nation and building our future together."

HUBBIE
BUBBA

on family

"I want an America that does more than talk about family values.

I want an America that values families."

—Notre Dame University. September 11th, 1992.

"Hillary and I, we're doing fine.
We're working on what we need to be working on,
and we're fine."

—A solid public image. At a fundraiser for Democrats. The *Boston Herald*. September 18, 1998.

"Think about

Mother's Day.

What is Mother's Day about? It's about love, discipline, values, and making someone think they are more important to somebody else than anybody in the world."

—Just for one day. Then it's back to ignoring. San Francisco, California.

May 11th, 1992.

The press has a way of finding out everything about you if you become President. President Reagan loved jelly beans; and President Bush didn't like broccoli; and last week the *Wall Street Journal* reported our dark secret that Hillary and I are addicted to salsa. And it all happened because of you—because we stayed up all night living on that before the election.

—Now pass that syringe over here. It's full of Old El Paso Chunky Style. Albuquerque, New Mexico. December 4th, 1993.

"It is important to me

that everybody who has been hurt know that the sorrow I feel is genuine: first and most important, my family; also my friends, my staff, my Cabinet, Monica Lewinsky and her family, and the American people. I have asked all for their forgiveness."

—Genuine? At the annual White House prayer breakfast.
The East Room. September 11th, 1998.

"Now,"

this matter is between me, the two people I love most—my wife and our daughter—and our God. I must put it right, and I am prepared to do whatever it takes to do so."

—Presidential families have their own private deity. Address to the Nation. August 18th, 1998

"And I say to you that while I know we have not always agreed and we'll never always agree on everything, I believe we share a common commitment to the working men and women and their children and their parents, the opportunity to dignity, to equality, and most of all to the forgotten middle class."

—What about the unforgotten no–class? Before the
AFL–CIO in Washington, DC. September 3rd, 1992.

"Most parents today have to work. We have no higher duty than to make sure that people who work and have children can be both successful at work and successful in the raising of their children—our most important job."

—Except those on welfare. But an end to that is near. Miami, Florida. September 19th, 1995.

"I did not have sexual relations with that woman.

I never told anybody to lie, not a single time. Never."

—Clinton's public statement early in the scandal, with Hillary at his side, 'nodding emphatically.' The *Buffalo News*. January 26th, 1998.

"And I want to be open with you. I want you to understand these have been the toughest days of my life. But they may turn out to be the most valuable for me and my family. And I have no one to blame but myself for my self–inflicted wounds. But that's not what America is about. And it doesn't take away from whether we're right or wrong on the issues or what we've done for the last six years or what this election's about. So what I want to say to you is you've been kind and understanding to me today. I hope you'll tell your friends and neighbors that I'm grateful, and that I am determined to redeem the trust of all the American people."

—"And I want to tell you about a great thing called Amway." At a fund–raiser for Lieutenant Governor Buddy Mackay. September 9th, 1998.

" Every year I ask all my relatives to gather with my wife's family at Christmastime. It is an amazing celebration of the different threads of family, a broad fabric of love and support that raised a child from modest means to a rewarding career in public life and a serious campaign for the Presidency."

—Cleveland, Ohio. May 21st, 1992.

"I misled people,
including even my wife. I deeply regret that… But it is private, and I intend to
reclaim my family life for my family. It's nobody's business but ours…
Even presidents have private lives."

—Enough about the privacy crap. It's all about the dirt. The *Buffalo News*. August 18th, 1998.

35 "I have waited for years

for my country to be once again in the position to build the future of our dreams for our children. I am grateful that this family has given so much to that end. But in the end, we rise or fall on the good judgment and the good service of the people. Do not blow this election. The best is still out there."

—Dinner for Kennedy Townsend. August 6th, 2000.

"We will celebrate the first Thanksgiving of the new millennium and the last one of our presidency. As Hillary and Chelsea and I sit down to our dinner, we will give special thanks for the privilege it has been to live here and to serve for the last eight years."

—And to all of the new stains on White House upholstery.
Reported in *New York Newsday*. November 23rd, 2000.

"The question is not, are family values important? Of course they are. It's not, are they under fire? Yes they are. It's not, is TV destructive of them? All too often it is. The question is: what are we going to do about it?"

—Lifetime Original programming on every station. Cleveland, Ohio. May 21st, 1992.

"She's a better

—You'll always be the best, Billy. In a *New York Times* interview, when the reporter told him that it's tough for a New York reporter to decide whether to cover him or Hillary. July 11th, 1999.

"Doing quite well considering what we've been through.

And God willing, we'll keep after it."

—The farce. On his marriage with Hillary following the sex scandals.
Reported in The Dominion (Wellington). April 3rd, 1999.

story now."

WILLIE KILLIE?

on war and peace

"If Iraq

came across the Jordan River, I would grab a
rifle and get in the trench and fight and die."

—At least two out of the three. To wild applause at a Jewish fund–raiser
in Toronto. Reported in the *New York Post*. August 2nd, 2002.

"We will make the U.S. the catalyst for a collective stand against aggression, the action I have urged in response to Serbian aggression in Bosnia…"

—Speech on foreign affairs. August 13th, 1992.

"I remember exactly what happened. Bruce Lindsey said to me on the phone, my God, a second plane has hit the tower. And I said, bin Laden did this. That's the first thing I said."

—Fists pounding on a desk, screaming to the sky, "bin Laaaaaadin!!!" *Larry King Live*. September 3rd, 2002.

"The U.S. military mission is not now nor was it ever one of nation building."

—But nation destroying, that's a whole other story.
Somalia message to Congress. October 13th, 1993.

"The guy is smart.

He's got access to money.

He's got a lot of the fanatic supporters around the world,

and has to be completely defeated and eradicated."

—Sick the robots from *Dr. Who* on bin Laden. "Exterminate. Exterminate."
Larry King Live. September 3rd, 2002.

"But our job is to see, if you will, from a different perspective the positions of both the Palestinians and the Israelis. You know, we—it's sort of like standing too close to an Impressionist painting sometime; there's lots of dots on the canvas, and the people who are standing too close to it, even though they're painting the canvas, may get lost in the weeds. And then the people that are standing back can see the picture, and it's a beautiful picture, if it all gets painted."

—Whoa. That's deep and pointless. Talking about America's involvement in the Mid-East peace process. *The News Hour with Jim Lehrer.* January 21st, 1998.

"The fact is America remains the indispensable nation. There are times when America, and only America, can make a difference between war and peace, between freedom and repression, between hope and fear. Of course, we can't take on all the world's burden. We cannot become its policemen. But where our interests and values demand it and where we can make a difference, America must act and lead. Nowhere is that responsibility more clear or more urgent than in the struggle against terrorism. No one is immune, whether you're riding a subway in Tokyo or a bus in Tel Aviv, whether you're window shopping in London or walking the streets in Moscow, whether you're doing your duty in Saudi Arabia or going to work in Oklahoma City. Terrorism has become an equal opportunity destroyer, with no respect for borders."

—George Washington University. Washington DC. August 5th, 1996.

"So, you know, this may sound naïve to all of you, but I can tell you, you know, I've ordered people into battle, I've dropped bombs, I've done all those things that you're supposed to do in the real world, usually to good effect. I'm proud of what we did in Bosnia and Kosovo."

—Is that what you're supposta do in the real world? UC Berkeley. January 29th, 2002.

"If Milosevic will not make peace, we will limit his ability to make war."

—After NATO airstrikes began in Serbia. Reported in the Baltimore Sun. March 25th, 1999.

Clinton: Yes. I thought that my virtual obsession with him was well–faced, and I was full of regret that I didn't get him. I mean, I immediately thought that he had done it.

King: You were obsessed with him?

Clinton: Yes I was. Some people thought I was obsessed?

—"I've got posters on my wall, bin Laden's Greatest Hits Volumes 1, 2 and 3…" Discussing bin Laden. *Larry King Live*. September 3rd, 2002.

"I don't think that.
I don't think September 11th had to happen at all,
and I will never be reconciled with the fact that it did."

—UC Berkeley. January 29th, 2002.

"I believe that there will still be rogue states that want nuclear, chemical, and biological weapons. I, furthermore, believe that there will be enemies of all nation states—terrorist groups, organized criminals, drug runners—who will be increasingly likely to have access to miniaturized, but powerful weapons of mass destruction. And what I would like to leave office doing is not getting credit for anything—I don't give a rip who gets the credit for it. What I want is the Chemical Weapons Convention to be enforced, the Biological Weapons Convention to have teeth added to it so it actually means something, and this Comprehensive Test Ban Treaty to be in place so at least we have a shot to reduce the number of nuclear states and the sophistication of their weapons and their ability to use them. That's the whole deal with me."

—Press conference at the White House. October 8th, 1999.

"And I wish I had been successful in my efforts to get Mr. Bin Laden earlier. But in the end, in the end, what's going to determine the shape of the 21st century, is whether we have an ethic that says, 'I think we like our differences. We like who we are. We like the color of our skin, the way we pursue our faith, we like what's about us that's different. We like our little boxes, we all have to have them to navigate reality.'"

—Yes Bill, 'our little boxes'… UC Berkeley. January 29th, 2002.

DOLLA BILL, YO, DOLLA, DOLLA BILL

on the economy

"And there is no country in the world as well-positioned for the global economy as we are, managing its diversity as well, giving different people opportunities and all we've got to do is to figure out that we've just got to keep working together, keep pulling together and keep going forward. Our best days are still ahead of us..."

—Washington DC. June 5th, 1996.

"**Probably**
there are people in this room
still mad at me at that budget
because you think I raised
your taxes too much. It
might surprise you to
know that I think I
raised them too
much too."

—Sly remarks at a Houston fund–raiser.
October 17th, 1995.

"In

"It's time to end the welfare system as we know it."

—And make the poor really suffer for their idleness. Speaking at the Clayton County Office of Family and Children's Services. September 11th, 1992.

a few moments, I will sign three agreements that will complete our negotiations with Mexico and Canada to create a North American Free Trade Agreement. In the coming months I will submit this pack to Congress for approval. It will be a hard fight, and I expect to be there with all of you every step of the way."

—Upon signing the NAFTA side agreements. The East Room. September 14th, 1993.

QUESTION Would you agree with me that the insertion of an object into the genitalia of another person with the desire to gratify sexually would fit within the definition you used in the Jones case as sexual relations?

CLINTON There is nothing here about that, is there? I don't know that I ever thought about that.

All I can tell you is whatever I thought was covered and I thought about this carefully. And let me just point out, this was uncomfortable for me. I had to acknowledge, because of this definition, that under this definition I had actually had sexual relations once with Gennifer Flowers, a person who had spread all kinds of ridiculous, dishonest, exaggerated stories about me for money. And I knew when I did that it would be leaked. It was. And I was embarrassed.

QUESTION And you're declining to answer the hypothetical about insertion of an object. I need to inform you, Mr. President that the grand jury will consider your not answering the questions more directly in their determination of whether or not they're going to issue another subpoena.

CLINTON Look, I'm not trying to be evasive here. I'm trying to protect my privacy, my family's privacy, and I'm trying to stick to what the deposition was about.

Grand Jury testimony. August 17th, 1998.

"Now,

if you look at the economy, we tried it our way for eight years. Before that, we tried it their way for 12 years, the deficit way. Our way works better, you know?"

—By using calculators, not abacuses. New York Senate 2000 Reception. October 23rd, 2000.

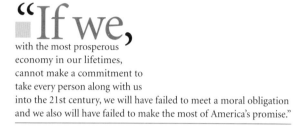

"If we, with the most prosperous economy in our lifetimes, cannot make a commitment to take every person along with us into the 21st century, we will have failed to meet a moral obligation and we also will have failed to make the most of America's promise."

—I think Huey Lewis was left behind. He still looks and acts very much 1987. Hazard, Kentucky. July 5th, 1999.

"Gary Winnick has been a friend of mine for some time now and I'm quite thrilled by the success that Global Crossing has had. And it's interesting to me and I think it's fitting that they're now housed in this historic site."

—Sing Sing. Beverly Hills, California. November 3rd, 2000.

"Well, first of all,

we are cutting spending.

We are cutting spending.

This idea that we're raising taxes—

we're putting in the—

taxes come in constant amounts.

If you put in—

whether it's a fuel tax or

an income tax."

—Taxing delivery during a conference call with
newspaper editorial boards. August 2nd, 1993.

imperfe

"And we cannot go into the global economy of the 21st century by walking away from our common responsibilities and saying that we don't have a common responsibility to help everybody's kids live up to the fullest of their dreams. You think about it, talk about it, stand up for it, work for it. Don't be overconfident and we will prevail."

—At a Democratic National Committee gala. Washington, DC. May 9th, 1996.

"In an imperfect world, we have something which will enable us to go forward together and to create a future that is worthy of our children and grandchildren, worthy of the legacy of America, and consistent with what we did at the end of World War II. We have to do that again. We have to create a new world economy."

—Upon signing the NAFTA side agreements. The East Room. September 14th, 1993.

QUESTION Do you agree with me that the statement, 'I was never alone with her,' is incorrect? You were alone with Monica Lewinsky, weren't you?

CLINTON Well, again... it depends on how you define alone. Yes, we were alone from time to time, even during 1997, even when there was absolutely no improper contact occurring. Yes, that is accurate. But there were also a lot of times when, even though no one could see us, the doors were open to the halls, on both ends of the halls, people could hear. The Navy stewards could come in and out at will, if they were around. ...So there were a lot of times when we were alone, but I never really thought we were.

—Grand Jury testimony. August 17th, 1998.

"But always before, after a period when the economy started to grow again, we got rid of it, and instead, I think because we were in the grip of an ideology that said government is always the problem, it will mess up a two—car parade, you should never, ever do anything that increases revenues or does anything about this deficit, we built in these huge interest rates and serious, serious imbalances in our economy."

—At a Democratic National Committee "mix and mingle" in New York. February. 24th, 2000.

"I see some of you out there who were at the White House Conference on Small Business. That was one of the highlights of my presidency when I got to read the federal regulation on grits. Remember that? That conference nearly made a liar out of me. I told you we were getting rid of 16,000 pages of federal regulations than we are, but it turned out the regulation on grits was one of the hardest ones to get rid of. We got one letter from a businessman—I read it actually—pleading with me not to get rid of the regulation on grits, saying that people would just be desperate trying to sort out the different kinds of corn necessary to make grits. If I hadn't been living on grits since I was an infant, I might not have had the sense to resist the intrigue to keep the regulation."

—Gritty remarks in Washington DC. June 5th, 1996.

Member of Audience: My question is, can you name one country that has ever taxed and spent itself back into prosperity? Thank you.

The President: The answer to your question is, I can't.

—Can you, huh, tough guy? Town Hall Meeting in San Diego, California. May 17th, 1993.

"I challenge a new generation of young Americans to a season of service—to act on your idealism by helping troubled children, keeping company with those in need, reconnecting our torn communities. There is much to be done—enough for millions of others who are still young in spirit to give of themselves in service, too. In serving, we recognize a simple but powerful truth: we need each other. And we must care for one another."

—First Inaugural speech, Washington, DC. January 20th, 1993.

"When I was alone with Ms. Lewinsky on certain occasions in early 1996, and once in early 1997, I engaged in conduct that was wrong. These encounters did not consist of sexual intercourse. They did not constitute sexual relations, as I understood that term to be defined at my January 17th, 1998 deposition. But they did involve inappropriate, intimate contact. These inappropriate encounters ended at my insistence in early 1997. I also had occasional telephone conversations with Ms. Lewinsky that included inappropriate sexual banter. I regret that what began as a friendship came to include this conduct. And I take full responsibility for my actions."

—Grand Jury testimony. August 17th, 1998.

"Let us begin by recognizing the fundamental reality that private enterprise, not government action, is the engine of economic growth and job creation. Our vision of the good society depends as much on a thriving private sector as anything else. Let us also recognize that there are things that government can and should do—give our private sector the tools to grow, and prepare our people for the jobs of the new economy."

—At G–7 Jobs Conference. Detroit, Michigan. March 14th, 1994.

"'The

third

"The third agreement answers one of the primary attacks on NAFTA that I heard for a year, which is, well, you can say all this, but something might happen that you can't foresee. Well, that's a good thing; otherwise we never would have had yesterday. I mean, I plead guilty to that."

—Philosophically mind bending. Upon signing the NAFTA side agreements.
The East Room. September 14th, 1993.

WILD BILL (AND) HIS—COCK

on women

"I wouldn't restrict myself to having just half the Cabinet be women.

I might want more."

—Rename it 'The Closet' and have mandatory 60 seconds in heaven sessions on a weekly basis. Democratic national debate. Reported in the *Boston Globe*. March 2nd, 1992.

"It's no secret to anybody that

I hoped that this relationship

would never become public."

—Speaking about his relationship with Monica Lewinsky. Grand Jury testimony. August 17th, 1998.

"I think I have been quite specific, and I think I've been willing to answer some specific questions that I haven't been asked yet, but I do not want to discuss something that is intensely painful to me. This has been tough enough already on me and on my family, although I take responsibility for it. I have no one to blame but myself."

—"It's hard on... er, difficult for everyone." Grand Jury testimony. August 17th, 1998.

"You know, if I were a single man, I might ask that mummy out. That's a good–looking mummy!"

—And you thought necrophilia was dead! Referring to 'Juanita', a recently discovered Incan mummy. *Time* Magazine. June 17th, 1996.

"A very large number of the people I have met in the last two days, especially young women, have asked me about her, so I thought I would introduce her, and I thank you for that."

—Reluctant to introduce Hillary in front of so many lovely young women.
Live telecast to the Russian people. Moscow. January 14th, 1994.

"**Female Reporter:** Mr. President, there's a move on Capitol Hill among some right–wing senators—Faircloth of North Carolina and also joined by—and D'Amato, of course, New York—and several left–wing Democrats, real liberal left–wing Democrats to try to get you out of office this month. They're going to try to do that by embarrassing you so that you will resign. Would you resign your office under any circumstances?

The President: Well, if you promise to run off with me, I might. But otherwise I can't think of any reason."

—At a press conference. August 10th, 1995.

QUESTION Your—that statement is a completely false statement. Whether or not Mr. Bennett knew of your relationship with Ms. Lewinsky, the statement that there was no sex of any kind in any manner, shape or form with President Clinton was an utterly false statement. Is that correct?

CLINTON It depends upon what the meaning of the word is means. If is means is, and never has been, that's one thing. If it means, there is none, that was a completely true statement.

Grand Jury testimony. August 17th, 1998.

"Do you want
to come into the

back office?"

—The invitation Monica Lewinsky claims Clinton gave her at their first
sexually charged encounter. The *San Francisco Chronicle*. March 1st, 2002.

"You know, tonight, before I went to the dinner that I previously attended, I met with about 16 or 17 women from the greater Denver area—all different kinds of women… and I felt so good when it was over because they were such impressive people and they represented what I am hoping we can bring to all the American people."

—Reception for the Saxophone Club. Denver, Colorado. July 22nd, 1996.

"We have tried to involve women at an unprecedented level."

—Waist high. Talking about the large number of women working in his administration. Washington, DC. May 1st, 1995.

r 17

"I remember very clearly about six or seven years ago when I had two events occur within two days, when I knew I was getting older. My hair had begun to gray, but I thought I was still in reasonably good shape. I felt fairly chipper. And I was making the rounds in my state and this beautiful young girl, whose parents were very close friends of mine and, therefore, I felt that I almost had a hand in her upbringing from the time she was born—she was 18 or 19 years old and she was nearly six feet tall. And she was just beautiful. And she came up to me—I was so pleased to see her—she came up to me and threw her arm around me, looked me straight in the eye, and she said, "Governor, you look so good for a man your age."

—At the White House Conference on Aging, Washington, DC. May 3rd, 1995.

"The truth is that most of the time, even when she was expressing her feelings for me in affectionate terms, I believe that she had accepted, understood my decision to stop this inappropriate contact. She knew from the very beginning of our relationship that I was apprehensive about it. And I think that in a way she felt a little freer to be affectionate, because she knew that nothing else was going to happen. I can't explain entirely what was in her mind. But most of these messages were not what you would call over the top. They weren't things that if you read them, you would say, oh my goodness, these people are having some sort of sexual affair."

—Grand Jury testimony. August 17th, 1998.

UNBILL-IEVABLE!

others on Clinton

"It was the same way people will cher-
ish a sweaty T–shirt from a rock star."

—Monica Lewinsky, on her rationale for idolizing her blue dress, which was creamed
with Clinton's wad. Reported in the *San Francisco Chronicle*. March 1st, 2002.

"Bill Clinton has none of it. He has not a creative bone in his body. Therefore, he's a bore, and will always be a bore… We all look forward with great pleasure to four years of wonderful, inspiring speeches, full of wit, poetry, music, love, and affection, plus more goddamned nonsense."

Peter Jennings interrupted with, "You can't say that on the air, Mr. Brinkley."

—David Brinkley. On ABC's election night coverage. November 6th, 1996.

"I was giving him a hip–hop kind of rap. I was like, 'Yo, how you gonna pay your bills? You can make a lot of money, you're Bill Clinton.' And you know what? He kept talking about Kosovo. Every time I talked about business, he'd talk about raising money for something that had to be done. The man's a do–gooder."

—Russell Simmons, chairman of Def Jam Records.
Reported in *New York* Magazine. September 18th, 2000.

"Mr. Clinton, sir. Americans didn't trust you with our health care systems. Americans didn't trust you with gays in the military. America doesn't trust you with our 21–year–old daughters, and we sure, Lord, don't trust you with our guns!"

—Charlton Heston at the NRA Annual Meeting, June 1998.

QUESTION Do you recall denying any sexual relationship with Monica Lewinsky to the following people Harry Thomason, Erskine Bowles, Harold Ickes, Mr. Podesta, Mr. Blumenthal, Mr. Jordan, Ms. Betty Currie?

CLINTON I recall telling a number of those people that I didn't have either I didn't have an affair with Monica Lewinsky or I didn't have sex with her. And I believe, sir, that you will have to ask them what they thought. But I was using those terms in the normal way people use them.

And so I said to them things that were true about this relationship. I said there is nothing going on between us. That was true. I said I have not had sex with her, as I define it. That was true.

Grand Jury testimony. August 17th, 1998.

"If he weren't the president of the United States and representing the cause of righteousness in the world, I would say, 'Man, go for it. Live it up. Do what you want.' But he represents something larger than just one human being. There are a lot of people who feel he has pissed on the office and denigrated it."

—Bruce Willis. *George* Magazine, August 1998.

"I'd rather say I despise him. I think hatred is a form of respect, after all. I have nothing but bottomless contempt for the President...
But I am getting to hate him."

—Christopher Hitchens, on MSNBC. Reported in the *Washington Times*. May 19th, 1999.

"The President's essential character flaw isn't dishonesty so much as a–honesty. It isn't that Clinton means to say things that are not true, or that he cannot make true, but that everything is true for him when he says it, because he says it. Clinton means what he says when he says it, but tomorrow he will mean what he says when he says the opposite. He is the existential President, living with absolute sincerety in the passing moment."

—Michael Kelly. "The President's Past". *New York Times Magazine.* July 31, 1994.

"It would be the equivalent of having the prime minister of England invite the Oklahoma City bombers to 10 Downing Street, to congratulate them on a job well done."

—Former British Prime Minister Margaret Thatcher responding to President Clinton's red-carpet welcome for Sinn Fein leader Gerry Adams. *Newsweek*. May 15th, 1995.

"Bill Clinton has been a true leader of the western world. He has been a friend and a counsel to me and other leaders right around the world."

—Tony Blair. Reported in the *New York Times*. December 15th, 2000.

"To begin with, I must respectfully disagree with the President's contention that his relationship with Monica Lewinsky and the way in which he misled us about it is nobody's business but his family's and that even Presidents have private lives, as he said. Whether he or we think it fair or not, the reality is in 1998 that a President's private life is public.

He failed to clearly articulate to the American people that he recognized how significant and consequential his wrongdoing was and how badly he felt about it.

He failed to show, I think, that he understood his behavior had diminished the office he holds and the country he serves and that it is inconsistent with the mainstream American values that he has advanced as President."

—Senator Joseph Libermann. From a speech about the Clinton–Lewinsky episode that was delivered on the Senate floor. September 4th, 1998.

"Bill Clinton would have played the Jew's harp stark naked on '60 Minutes' if he thought it would get him elected. He is the Willy Loman of Generation X, a traveling salesman who has the loyalty of a lizard with his tail broken off and the midnight taste of a man who'd double date with the Rev. Jimmy Swaggart."

—Hunter S. Thompson. Reported in the *South Bend Tribune*. September 6th, 1998.

"Probably the main thing about him is that he drew the Democratic Party back into the majority mainstream—with all the positive and negative implications of that."

—Arthur Miller. The *New York Times*. December 27th, 2000.

"…does it seem right that this exceptional human being should be prevented from fulfilling his historical destiny simply because he was unable to find a private place to make love? That is just what happened. The most powerful man in the world was kept from consummating his secret passions by the invisible presence of a Secret Service that served as much to restrain as to protect."

—Gabriel Garcia Marquez. *Salon.* February 1st, 1999.

"Keep your voice up, Mr. President."

—Clinton's attorney, Robert Bennett, heard from the sidelines as the camera focuses on Clinton in his videotaped testimony in the Paula Jones case. Bennett's encouragement comes just after Clinton denies having an affair with Ms. Jones. *New York Daily News*. December 11, 1998.

"For our children, resign."

—A protest sign seen outside a fundraiser Clinton was attending. The *Boston Herald*. September 18, 1998.

QUESTION If Monica Lewinsky says that you used a cigar as a sexual aid with her in the Oval Office area, would she be lying? Yes, no, or won't answer?

CLINTON I will revert to my former statement.

QUESTION If Monica Lewinsky says that you had phone sex with her, would she be lying?

CLINTON Well, that is at least, in general terms, I think, is covered by my statement.

QUESTION Let me define phone sex for purposes of my question. Phone sex occurs when the party to the phone conversation masturbates while the other party is talking in a sexually explicit manner. The question is, if Monica Lewinsky says that you had phone sex with her, would she be lying?

CLINTON I think that is covered by my statement.

Grand Jury testimony. August 17th, 1998.

"There is a difference between a woman able to make a conscious decision to tolerate something like this for a higher reason, and a woman who feels like she has to 'take it' off him. I don't think anybody thinks Hillary would fall into that second category."

—Martha Burke, a political psychologist with the Centre for Advancement of Public Policy in Washington. The *Daily Telegraph*. August 21st, 1998.

"He just sort of looked at me in this way that sort of gave me the full–on Bill Clinton. And I responded. I flirted back."

—Not that it meant anything. Monica Lewinsky in her HBO special, *Monica in Black and White*. Reported in the *San Francisco Chronicle*. March 1st, 2002.

"Four more years!"

—The chant taken up by a Clinton audience of 2000 in a high school gym, just nine days before he was to leave office. They all failed social studies that semester. Reported in the *Boston Herald*. January 12th, 2001.

"President Clinton's an unusually good liar. Unusually good. Do you realize that?"

—Senator Bob Kerrey's assessment of Clinton in *Esquire* magazine. Reported in the *Boston Globe*. August 16th, 1998.

"From what I've heard, a lot of Bill Clinton's women have been satisfied customers."

—Robert Wright, the Donaghey Distinguished Law Professor at the University of Arkansas law school at Little Rock. The *Toronto Star*. April 2, 1998.

"Two words were not being spoken much at the Democrat's convention in Los Angeles: 'Monica' and 'Willard'. Monica needs neither introduction nor explanation, but Willard maybe does; it's the name Bill Clinton gave to his penis, according to another of his women, Gennifer Flowers. Clinton's reasoning: 'It's longer than Willie.'"

—From an entertainment review. *The Observer*. August 20th, 2000.

"We ought to give credit where credit is due, and I do want to thank Bill Clinton for everything he's done to remind people what they like about Republicans."

—RNC Chairman Haley Barbour, opening Remarks at RNC Winter Meetings. San Diego, California. January 20th, 1996.

"Trailer trash."

—What Clinton allegedly urged James Carville, his P.R. guy, and Bob Bennett, his lawyer, to label Paula Jones. *USA Today.* September 23rd, 1998.

Reporter: Your Majesty, you had the opportunity to meet seven Presidents of the United States. How did you find the President Bill Clinton different of the other? Thank you.

King Hassan(of Morocco): First, let me say that no two men are alike. As a wise man once said, style is what defines the man. All the different presidents that I've had the honor to meet here contribute together to the richness and the variety in the United States. Each time it has been a new style, a new inspiration, a new team.

President Clinton: If His Majesty had not been a direct descendent of the Prophet, he might have become Morocco's greatest diplomat.

—President Clinton and King Hassan of Morocco at a White House Press Conference. Washington, DC. March 15th, 1995.

"We black people have gone through eight years and have been shown options because Mr. Clinton was president. He was very effective; there was an economic boom in a certain part of America. The black people had the opportunity to take advantage of the options. He was a little more open than other presidents. We perceived him as being cool—I wouldn't say whether he was or wasn't. For black people, it was good and bad. His being cool lulled a lot of us into sleep. Over all, he was a man who did his job. The mainstream—the white American public—ostracized him for the things that he did that had no bearing on his job."

—Chuck D. The *New York Times*. December 27th, 2000.

"Let's go to the other candidate, the Governor of Arkansas who's managing a population for 12 years—12 years he's been running a population the size of Dallas and Fort Worth."

—Ross Perot. In a TV commercial aired on November 2nd, 1992.

"Make no mistake, the judgment of history does matter. It matters profoundly. And impeachment by the full House has already brought profound disgrace to President Clinton. Whatever happens now will do little to affect history's judgment of him."

—Former Presidents Gerald Ford and Jimmy Carter, urging censure for President Clinton. *Chicago Tribune*, December 22nd, 1998.

SO LONG, BUB

BUB

closing remarks

"The American people have now spoken, but it's going to take a little while to determine exactly what they said."

—Reported in *New York Newsday*. November 9th, 2000.

"In
all the work I have done as president, every decision I have made, every executive action I have taken, every bill I have proposed and signed, I've tried to give all Americans the tools and conditions to build the future of our dreams, in a good society, with a strong economy, a cleaner environment, and a freer, safer, more prosperous world."

—Farewell address. January 19th, 2001.

QUESTION The grand jury would like to know, Mr. President, why it is that you think that oral sex performed on you does not fall within the definition of sexual relations as used in this deposition.

CLINTON Because that is if the deponent is the person who has oral sex performed on him, then the contact is with not with anything on that list, but with the lips of another person. It seems to be self—evident that that's what it is. And I thought it was curious.

Let me remind you, sir, I read this carefully. And I thought about it. I thought about what "contact" meant. I thought about what "intent to arouse or gratify" meant. And I had to admit under this definition that I'd actually had sexual relations with Gennifer Flowers. Now, I would rather have taken a whipping than done that, after all the trouble I'd been through with Gennifer Flowers, and the money I knew that she made for the story she told…

Grand Jury testimony.
August 17th, 1998.

"Oh God,

I hated running against him because I like him so much."

—"Isn't that right, pookie?" Talking about Bob Dole. *Larry King Live*. September 3rd, 2002.

"In a funny way,
when you realize there's nothing left to hide,
it sort of frees you up to do what
you ought to do anyway."

—Like licking snow cones and poodle sculpting. Discussing his counseling sessions to
4000 church members. Reported in the *New York Times*. August 11th, 2000.

"I know the Chinese and the Indians often believed when I was president that–they liked me well enough and they thought I meant them well–but when I got off on this, they thought I was either going into never–never land or I had some Machiavellian strategy to keep them poor."

—Talking about his strategy for raising the poverty level in developing countries without destroying the environment. UC Berkeley. January 29th, 2002.

toxicity of

"…all the medical studies now show that the toxicity of marijuana available today breaks up the concentration patterns of young people, can threaten the ability of young women to give birth to normal children, can undermine the whole future of people."

—Minneapolis, Minnesota. October 28th, 1996.

"I think that most small amounts of marijuana have been de–criminalized in most places and should be."

—After being told the interview would not be published until after the 2000 election. Interview for *Rolling Stone*. November 11th, 2000.

"And

we just voted to extend the Brady Bill to say if you beat up your spouse or you child, you can't get a gun, either. And I think we were right again."

—Bullsheeeeeeeeeet! Wives and children need a good pistol whippin' every once in a while. It's in the constitution. Minneapolis, Minnesota. October 28th, 1996.

"Yes, I'd like to have you come on my show. But I've got a lot of questions I always wanted to ask you."

—Mostly about divorce settlements. Talking about getting his own talk show. *Larry King Live*. September 3rd, 2002.

"I do not believe you can solve complex questions at the grass roots level or at the national level or anywhere in between if you have too much extremism of rhetoric and excessive partisanship. Times are changing too fast. We need to keep our eyes open. We need to keep our ears open. We need to be flexible. We need to have new solutions based on old values. I just don't think we can get there unless we can establish some common ground."

—Georgetown University. July 6th, 1995.

"Hunters must always be free to hunt. Law–abiding adults should always be free to own guns to protect their homes. I respect that part of our culture, I grew up in it. But I want to ask the sportsmen and others who lawfully own guns to join us in this campaign to reduce gun violence. I say to you, I know you didn't create this problem, but we need your help to solve it."

—Heeeeeeeeeee hawwwwwwwwwwww! Talking about the Brady Law. Second Inaugural Address. January 20th, 1997.

QUESTION Mr. President, among the many remaining questions of the grand jurors is one that they would like answered directly without relation to, without regard to inferences, which is the following: Did Monica Lewinsky perform oral sex on you? They would like a direct answer to that, yes or no?

CLINTON Well, that's not the first time that question's been asked. But since I believe, and I think any person, reasonable person would believe that that is not covered in the definition of sexual relations I was given, I'm not going to answer, except to refer to my statement."

Grand Jury Testimony. August 17th, 1998.

"Almost

makes you

want to go to

jail out here, doesn't it?"

—Who brought the whips and chains 'cause it's time for a little role playin'. When visiting a hill-top castle/prison in Mallorca, Spain. Reported in the *St. Louis Post–Dispatch*. July 6th, 1997.

"

Throughout our history, any leader who raised strong hopes and wanted to make big changes has tended to spark an adverse reaction too, just almost like a law of physics. If you're moving strongly in one direction, you will have an equal and opposite force in the other direction."

—On threats against his life, in an interview with Tom Brokaw on *NBC Nightly News*. January 26th, 1995.

"Great does not always mean good, but at least it's large."

—Huh? Talking about how Russia will define itself in the 21st century. Huh? Live telecast to the Russian people. Moscow. January 14th, 1994.

"What I want the American people to know, what I want the Congress to know is that I am profoundly sorry for all I have done wrong in words and deeds. I never should have misled the country, the Congress, my friends or my family. Quite simply, I gave in to my shame."

—Tell it to the judge. Oh, you did. Talking about misleading the American people about his affair with Monica Lewinsky. At the same time, he maintained that he never lied under oath. The *Tampa Tribune*. December 12, 1998.

"I think

it is a legitimate thing for countries—other countries to ask the United States to do more to reduce its demand for drugs. We have roughly five percent of the world's population; we consume roughly half of the world's illegal drugs. So I think that's a legitimate thing."

—Put that in your pipe and smoke it. With president Zedillo of Mexico. Old Executive Office Building. October 5th, 1995.

"After eight years and with exactly nine days to go,
the last dog **is still barking.**"

—Referring to his promise to stand by the American people, despite
his scandals. Reported in the *Boston Herald*. January 12, 2001.

"But the paradox is—
let me just give you the paradox—

the paradox is a year or so ago, Hillary and I went to Riga, Latvia, to celebrate the withdrawal of Russian troops there for the first time since before World War II; tens of thousands of people in the street weeping with joy, loving America. A poll just came out and said that Bill Clinton was the most popular politician in Latvia. I'm trying to figure out how to get on the ballot there, give them some electoral votes."

—On his popularity, at "America's Hope, Arkansas Pride" Luncheon. Little Rock, Arkansas. June 23rd, 1995.

"Now we have to do what your generation did for us, to guide new democracies into an era of security and prosperity, to renew our own economy, to give hope to our communities, to give every individual the tools they need to assume personal responsibility for themselves and their families, to prepare our young people for life in the 21st century. And perhaps still most difficult of all, we have got to find a way to work together in this country to make a strength out of our diversity, to prove that in a global economy where the Earth is smaller and smaller, the fact that we are nations of many races and faiths and many backgrounds is a great source of strength if we will tap it with open minds and open hearts."

—Remarks honoring African–American Veterans of World War II. September 16th, 1994.

"I was an equal opportunity eater.
Every ethnic group got a shot."

—Fund–raiser for Rep. Dick Durbin's Senate bid. Touring the Taste of Chicago food fes-
tival, Clinton ate jerk chicken, cheeseburgers, fried Filipino egg rolls, barbecued pork,
pirogues, Tandoori chicken and rice, and cheese corn bread—then disappeared into
the Johnny–on–the–Spot for several minutes. Reported in *USA Today*. July 3rd, 1996.

"So what I want you to do is to go out of here and say, look, you may not agree with everything Bill Clinton and Al Gore do. I don't agree with everything Bill Clinton and Al Gore do."

—Like making pee monsters on the Capitol Building.
At the Florida Presidential Gala. September 19th, 1995.

"If you're not
you have this
kind of job,

"Mr. Wisenberg,

I have testified about this three times. Now, I will do it the fourth time. I am not going to answer your trick questions."

—"I am the king of trickery, and you will not dethrone me!" Grand Jury testimony. August 17th, 1998.

careful when

"If you're not careful when you have this kind of job, it can overtake you. You can believe it's even more important than it is. You can let it take up even more time than it should. It can crowd out all that other stuff that keeps you centered and growing and whole."

—Like Tae Bo and *Everybody Loves Raymond*. Speaking to 4000 church members. Reported in the *New York Times*. August 11th, 2000.

"As for me,

I'll leave the presidency more idealistic, more full of hope than the day I arrived and more confident than ever that America's best days lie ahead."

—And the best lies are days behind. Farewell address. January 19th, 2001.

"Some are funny
and some aren't."

—When asked what he thought of the 'Clinton' jokes.
MTV's *Enough is Enough*. April 19th, 1994.

"I've already talked longer than I meant to.
And I didn't have any idea what I was
going to say when I got here.
But I'm glad I got invited."

—To a women's group in Florida. October 4th, 2000.

"I think the most significant thing I have learned is that the President—being President and being an effective President and a good leader for our country is about more than actually what you accomplish. It's about more than the bills you pass in Congress or the executive actions you take. It's also about the words that you say and how you say them."

—On a *Larry King Radio Town Meeting*. September 21st, 1995.

"I have never had sexual relations with
Monica Lewinsky."

—Clinton's response to a question in the Paula Jones case.
Reported in the *Boston Globe*. April 13th, 1999.